LONGMAN INTEGRATED SKILLS

Boost!

Speaking 1

PEARSON
Longman

Jason Renshaw

Series Editors: Cecilia Petersen and Mayumi Tabuchi

Published by
Pearson Longman Asia ELT
20/F Cornwall House
Taikoo Place
979 King's Road
Quarry Bay
Hong Kong

fax: +852 2856 9578
email: pearsonlongman@pearsoned.com.hk
www.longman.com

and Associated Companies throughout the world.

First published 2007

Produced by Pearson Education Asia Limited, Hong Kong
GCC/01

ISBN-13: 978-962-00-5877-6
ISBN-10: 962-00-5877-1

Publisher: Simon Campbell
Senior Editor: Howard Cheung
Editor: Angela Cheung
Designers: Junko Funaki, Annie Chan
Illustrators: Balic Choy, Bernd Wong
Audio Production: David Pope and Sky Productions

For permission to use copyrighted images, we would like to thank © Tim OLeary/zefa/Corbis (pp. 5 BL, 13 TR and 18 TL), © Charles Gupton/ Corbis (p. 13 CL), © Ed Bock/Corbis (p. 15 BL), © Tom Stewart/Corbis (pp. 16 TR and 26 TR), © Gareth Brown/Corbis (p. 16 BR), © Frank Lukasseck/ zefa/Corbis (p. 32 TL), © Lowell Georgia/Corbis (p. 32 TR), © Denis Scott/Corbis (p. 35 TR), © David Pollack/Corbis (p. 41 TR), © Bruce Burkhardt/ Corbis (p. 56 TR), © Michael Nicholson/Corbis (p. 56 CL), © F. Carter Smith/Sygma/Corbis (p. 62 CR), © Roy Morsch/Corbis (p. 66 TR), © Freitag/ zefa/Corbis (p. 68 BL) and © Parque/zefa/Corbis (p. 68 BR).

Acknowledgements
The Boost! Speaking component is dedicated to some key people who have been instrumental in helping me grow as an EFL professional, namely Gordon Lewis, Jake Kimball and Andrew Wright. I'd also like to thank the many colleagues I've enjoyed discussing YL and Teenager educational issues with through Korea TESOL and the IATEFL Young Learners and Teenagers Special Interest Group.
Jason Renshaw

The Publishers would also like to thank the following teachers for their suggestions and comments on this course:
Tara Cameron, Rosanne Cerello, Nancy Chan, Chang Li Ping, Joy Chao, Jessie Chen, Josephine Chen, Chiang Ying-hsueh, Claire Cho, Cindy Chuang, Linda Chuang, Chueh Shiu-wen, Mark de Boer, Mieko Hayashida, Diana Ho, Lulu Hsu, Eunice Jung, Hye Ri Kim, Jake Kimball, Josie Lai, Carol Lee, Elaine Lee, Melody Lee, Peggy Li, Esther Lim, Moon Jeong Lim, Jasmin Lin, Martin Lin, Catherine Littlehale Oki, Linda Liu, Tammy Liu, Goldie Luk, Ma Li-ling, Chizuko Matsushita, Geordie McGarty, Yasuyo Mito, Eunice Izumi Miyashita, Mari Nakamura, Yannick O'Neill, Coco Pan, Hannah Park, Karen Peng, Zanne Schultz, Kaj Schwermer, Mi Yeon Shin, Giant Shu, Dean Stafford, Hyunju Suh, Tan Yung-hui, Devon Thagard, John and Charlie van Goch, Annie Wang, Wang Shu-ling, Wu Lien-chun, Sabrina Wu, Yeh Shihfen, Tom Yeh, Laura Yoshida and Yunji Yun.

Welcome to

Boost!
Speaking 1

The **Boost!** Skills Series is the definitive and comprehensive four-level series of skills books for junior EFL learners. The series has been developed around age-appropriate, cross-curricular topics that develop students' critical thinking and examination techniques. It follows an integrated skills approach with each of the skills brought together at the end of each unit.

The twelve core units in **Boost! Speaking 1** follow a clear and transparent structure to make teaching and learning easy and fun. The speaking skills build and progress across the four levels of **Boost! Speaking** and are correlated to the next generation of tests of English.

You will find the following in **Boost! Speaking 1**:

- Age-appropriate and cross-curricular topics
- Realistic and relevant contexts from students' lives
- A variety of dialogues and speeches for formal and informal speaking
- Pronunciation practice on sounds and stress patterns

Unit Topic

Each unit has an age-appropriate and cross-curricular topic.

Students will

- find the topic directly relates to their own lives and study.
- be engaged and motivated to learn.

Speaking Skill

A very simple introduction of the targeted unit skill is provided.

Students will

- be introduced to the speaking skill in a clear and understandable way.

Pronunciation Focus

Difficult sounds and stress patterns are presented to help students speak more accurately and confidently.

Students will

- be able to practice difficult sounds.
- learn how to stress key words and sentences.

Speaking Model

A model dialogue or speech is presented with a noticing task.

Students will

- be exposed to a variety of dialogues and speeches for formal and informal speaking.
- discover the speaking skill for themselves without the need for long explanations.

Audio CD

The CD at the back of the Student Book provides audio support for all dialogues and speeches plus the audio for the Integration listening tasks.

Speaking Practice

Key sentences that highlight the unit skill are practiced, together with substitutable words or phrases.

Students will

- develop the skills needed for accurate and effective speaking.
- be able to follow guidance to prepare and present their own dialogues or speeches.

Integration

The speaking skill is combined with listening, reading or writing tasks.

Students will

- prepare for an oral task based on reading and writing/listening inputs.
- develop language skills needed for the next generation of integrated tests of English.

Review

After every two core units there is a review which consolidates the speaking skills already studied.

Students will

- be able to see their progress in using speaking skills.
- build on previously taught skills to produce interesting and natural dialogues or speeches.

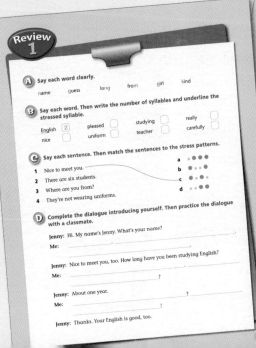

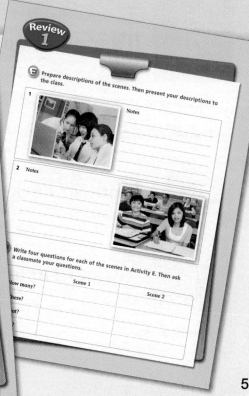

Contents

Evaluation

	Successful with the skill	Needs to review the skill	Comments
Unit 1 Introducing yourself			
Unit 2 Describing people			
Unit 3 Talking about activities (1)			
Unit 4 Talking about activities (2)			
Unit 5 Using polite phrases			
Unit 6 Describing things with facts			
Unit 7 Asking for clarification			
Unit 8 Saying what you prefer			
Unit 9 Using contractions			
Unit 10 Telling a story			
Unit 11 Giving instructions			
Unit 12 Expressing opinions in a debate			

Speaking Model

A 🎧 2 **Listen and read.**

Kin:	Hi! I'm Kin. What's your name?
Maria:	Hello. My name's Maria. Nice to meet you.
Kin:	Nice to meet you, too. Where are you from?
Maria:	I'm from Italy. I've been at this school for only two weeks. How about you?
Kin:	Oh, for about three years. How long have you been studying English?
Maria:	I started studying English in Rome about two years ago.
Kin:	Just two years ago? Your English is really good!
Maria:	Thanks. Your English is good, too.

B **Answer the questions and follow the instruction.**

1 What does Maria say to greet Kin?

2 Which line in the dialogue shows Kin is surprised?

3 Underline sentences where Kin and Maria say something nice about each other.

Speaking Skill

Introducing yourself

You can introduce yourself by saying hello and giving your name. You can be polite by saying *Nice to meet you.* or *Nice to see you.* and giving compliments (saying something nice about the person).

Speaking Practice

C 🎧 **3** **Listen and repeat. Then work with a classmate and take turns saying each sentence using the words given.**

1	Hi! I'm Kin. / Hello. My name's Maria.	[names]
2	How long have you been studying English?	learning French, playing the piano
3	Oh, for about three years.	two, five months, weeks
4	Your English is really good!	French, Spanish excellent, great

Pronunciation Focus

D 🎧 **4-6** **Listen and repeat.**

Sounds

name	meet	from
name	nice	been
long	studying	

Words

my   meet   nice
real·ly   Eng·lish
stud·y·ing   I·tal·y

Sentences

● ● ● ● ●
1 Nice to meet you, too.

● ● ● ●
2 Where are you from?

● ● ● ● ● ● ● ●
3 I've been at this school for only two weeks.

TIP For words, stress the highlighted syllable. For sentences, stress the words with bigger circles.

7 **Put the dialogue in the correct order. Then listen and practice the dialogue with a classmate.**

Mary: Yes, I've been coming to the music club for only a week. How about you? ☐

Tom: Thanks. You play the violin well, too. ☐

Mary: Wow, just two months? You play the trumpet very well! ☐

Tom: I'm Tom. Nice to meet you. You're new here, aren't you? ☐

Mary: Hi. My name's Mary. What's your name? ☐ 1

Tom: Oh, for about two months. ☐

 Work with a classmate. Prepare a dialogue introducing yourself to each other.

Useful words | drama club   science club   tennis club   practice   learn   great

Me: ____ Hi. My name's _____

Classmate: _____

_____

_____

_____

_____

_____

_____

G **Present your dialogue to the class.**

TIP Remember to make your dialogue polite by saying something nice about the person you are talking to.

Integration

H **Write your answers. Then ask two classmates the same questions and write their answers.**

1 Which activity are you going to do after school?

_____

_____

2 How long have you been doing it?

_____

_____

3 What other activities do you like doing?

_____

_____

Name: _____

1 _____

_____

2 _____

_____

3 _____

Name: _____

1 _____

_____

2 _____

_____

3 _____

TiP

Use these phrases to help you:
- Can you say that again, please?
- How do you spell that?

I **Tell the class about your classmates.**

In Class

Unit 2

Speaking Model

A 🎧 (8) **Listen and read.**

This is a classroom. There's a teacher and there are six students. The teacher is a man. He looks very pleased with his students. The students are wearing uniforms. One of them is reading something. I guess the others are listening. They look happy.

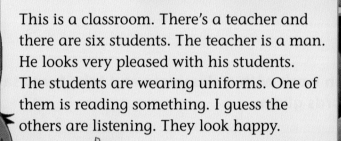

I believe this is an art room. I can see three students painting pictures on a big table. They're not wearing uniforms. The girl in the yellow shirt is mixing the paint carefully. All of the students look kind of serious.

B **Answer the question and follow the instruction.**

1 What do the girl and boy say about the scenes? (Check [✓] more than one answer)

When the action takes place ☐   What the people are saying ☐

Where the action takes place ✓   How the people look ☐

What the people are doing ☐

2 Circle an expression in each paragraph that has a similar meaning to "I think."

Speaking Skill

Describing people

When you describe people, you can talk about

- where they are.
- what they are doing.
- the way they look (expressions and moods).

Speaking Practice

C 🎧 9 **Listen and repeat. Then work with a classmate and take turns saying each sentence using the words given.**

1	There's a teacher.	a coach, a student
2	They look happy.	excited, serious
3	I believe this is an art room.	a music room, a science room
4	I can see three students painting pictures.	six children, two girls reading books, doing math

Pronunciation Focus

D 🎧 10-12 **Listen and repeat.**

Sounds

kind	look	carefully
girl	big	guess

Words

room   man   pleased
teach·er   list·en
u·ni·form   care·ful·ly

Sentences

1   There are six students.

2   They're not wearing uniforms.

3   All of the students look kind of serious.

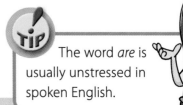

TIP
The word *are* is usually unstressed in spoken English.

14

⌂13 **Complete the description using the words from the box. Then listen and practice the description with a classmate.**

teacher	glasses	believe	looking	students	looks	yellow	There's

I (1)_____ this is a science room.

(2)_____ a teacher and there are four

(3)_____. The (4)_____

is a woman. The students are wearing special

(5)_____. They're (6)_____

at some (7)_____ liquid. Everyone

(8)_____ interested.

 Prepare a description of the scene. Then practice the description with a classmate.

Useful words   library   show   computer   interested   happy

Notes

_____

_____

_____

_____

_____

_____

_____

TIP Try to organize your sentences in a clear order.

 Present your description to the class.

Integration

H ▶ (14) **Read Suki's description of the scene. Then work with a classmate and take turns asking and answering the questions.**

I guess this is a soccer field. There are five students and they're all girls. There's also a coach. She's a woman. They're all sitting on the grass. The coach is saying something. The girls are all listening to her. They look kind of tired but they're all paying attention.

1 How many girls are there?

2 Where are they sitting?

3 How do the girls look?

4 What are the girls doing?

I **Choose a scene and prepare four questions about it. Then ask a classmate your questions.**

A    **B**

Scene ⬡

1 How many _____ ?

2 Where _____ ?

3 What _____ ?

4 How _____ ?

A Say each word clearly.

name   guess   long   from   girl   kind

B Say each word. Then write the number of syllables and underline the stressed syllable.

<u>Eng</u>lish ☐2   pleased ☐   studying ☐   really ☐

nice ☐   uniform ☐   teacher ☐   carefully ☐

C Say each sentence. Then match the sentences to the stress patterns.

1 Nice to meet you.   **a** ● ● ● ●

2 There are six students.   **b** ● ● ● ●

3 Where are you from?   **c** ● ● ● ●

4 They're not wearing uniforms.   **d** ● ● ● ●

D Complete the dialogue introducing yourself. Then practice the dialogue with a classmate.

Jenny: Hi. My name's Jenny. What's your name?

Me: _____. _____.

_____.

Jenny: Nice to meet you, too. How long have you been studying English?

Me: _____.

_____?

Jenny: About one year.

Me: _____?

_____!

Jenny: Thanks. Your English is good, too.

 E Prepare descriptions of the scenes. Then present your descriptions to the class.

1

Notes

_____

_____

_____

_____

2 Notes

_____

_____

_____

_____

_____

 F Write four questions for each of the scenes in Activity E. Then ask a classmate your questions.

		Scene 1	Scene 2
1	How many?		
2	Where?		
3	What?		
4	How?		

Speaking Model

A 🎧 15 **Listen and read.**

Sara:	Hi, Ken. What are you doing after school today?
Ken:	I've got some free time, so I'm going to play computer games at home.
Sara:	Oh, really? I like playing computer games, too.
Ken:	Which game do you like best?
Sara:	Hm … I like Battle Power a lot. It's really fun.
Ken:	Yeah. I love it, too.
Sara:	What else do you like playing?
Ken:	I enjoy playing Castle Park very much. It's my favorite now. It's pretty new. It's about flying in a future city.
Sara:	Wow, that sounds great.

B **Answer the question and follow the instructions.**

1 Which computer game do both Sara and Ken enjoy playing?

2 Circle the expression that shows Sara likes the same thing as Ken.

3 Underline two questions that ask for more information.

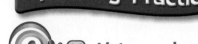

Speaking Skill

Talking about activities (1)

You can find out what people do in their free time by

- asking about their plans (*What are you doing after school today?*).
- talking about the things they like doing (*I like playing computer games, too*).
- asking specific information about the things they like doing (*Which game do you like best?*).

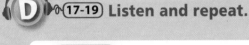

Speaking Practice

C 🎧 16 **Listen and repeat. Then work with a classmate and take turns saying each sentence using the words given.**

1	What are you doing after school today?	tomorrow, this weekend
2	Oh, really? I like playing computer games, too.	reading books, watching movies
3	Which game do you like best?	book, movie
4	I enjoy playing Castle Park very much.	reading comic books, watching cartoons

Pronunciation Focus

D 🎧 17-19 **Listen and repeat.**

Sounds

park	power
best	battle

Words

free   games   time
play·ing   en·joy   to·day
com·put·er   fa·vo·rite

Sentences

1   I'm going to play computer games at home.

2   What else do you like playing?

3   Wow, that sounds great.

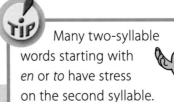

TIP Many two-syllable words starting with *en* or *to* have stress on the second syllable.

E 🎧 20 **Complete each line in the dialogue by matching the two parts. Then listen and practice the dialogue with a classmate.**

Mark: What are you doing ⟨ c ⟩

Ted: I'm going to watch ⟨ ⟩

Mark: Oh, really?
Spider-Man movies ⟨ ⟩

Ted: What other ⟨ ⟩

Mark: I like all the ⟨ ⟩

a are great.

b movies do you like?

c after soccer practice?

d Superman movies, too.

e the new Spider-Man movie.

F **Work with a classmate. Prepare a dialogue about your free time activities.**

Useful words	chat online listen to music go swimming do karate
	play the guitar play badminton play basketball

TIP
You could start by asking
what your classmate is going
to do after school today.

G **Present your dialogue to the class.**

Integration

H (21-22) **Read the notice. Then listen and complete the dialogue.**

Need something to do after school?

Why not join a club?

You can learn to play many kinds of musical instruments.

You can also enjoy sports like baseball and soccer.

All clubs meet on Mondays, Wednesdays and Fridays.

Laura: Hi, Sally. (1)_____ you seen this notice?

Sally: Yeah. I signed up yesterday.

Laura: Oh, (2)_____? Which club are you (3)_____ to join?

Sally: I really (4)_____ baseball, so I'm going to join that club.

Laura: Do you want to join (5)_____ music clubs?

Sally: No, I don't like music much. I (6)_____ enjoy playing sports.

Laura: Well, I like music. I'd like to learn how to (7)_____ the violin.

Sally: Why don't you sign up for the violin club, then?

Laura: I can't. I don't have (8)_____ time on those days.

I **Work with a classmate. Take turns asking and answering the questions.**

1 What is the school offering?

2 On what days can students do the activities?

3 Which club is Sally going to join?

4 Why can't Laura join any of the clubs?

It's a great sport!

Unit 4

Speaking Model

A 🎧 (23) **Listen and read.**

I think basketball is a great sport. All you need are a ball and a court. You can play it outdoors or inside a sports center. It's a team sport so it's fun to play with friends. You can play it after school or on the weekend. I like basketball because it's exciting and fun.

Well, I really enjoy skiing. You do it on snowy mountains. You can ski on weekends or during winter vacation. All you need are warm clothes, a pair of skis and ski poles. It's fun to ski with other people, such as your family or friends. I like skiing because it's fast and a bit dangerous.

B **Follow the instructions and answer the question.**

1 Circle the things that you need to do the sports.

2 Underline the places where you can do the sports.

3 Why does the boy like basketball?

Speaking Skill

Talking about activities (2)

When you talk about an activity you like doing, you can
- say what it is.
- give some details to describe it (how many players are needed, what you need to play it, where to play it).
- give some reasons to say why you like it.

Speaking Practice

C 🎧 **24** **Listen and repeat. Then work with a classmate and take turns saying each sentence using the words given.**

1	I think basketball is a great sport.	skiing, soccer good, wonderful
2	All you need are a ball and a court.	a racket and some balls
3	You can play it outdoors.	indoors, anywhere
4	It's fun to ski with other people.	exciting, great play soccer with friends

Pronunciation Focus

D 🎧 **25-27** **Listen and repeat.**

Sounds

skiing   sport   snowy

Words

great   court
cen·ter   moun·tains
ex·cit·ing   dan·ger·ous

Sentences

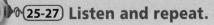

1 It's a team sport.

2 You can play it after school.

3 I like basketball because it's exciting and fun.

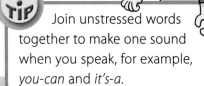

TIP Join unstressed words together to make one sound when you speak, for example, *you-can* and *it's-a*.

E 🎧 28 **Draw an arrow to show where each highlighted word should go in the sentence. Then listen and practice saying the paragraph with a classmate.**

1 Well, I hiking is a fun activity think.

2 All you are need hiking shoes and a backpack.

3 You can do any it time of the year.

4 You can do it weekends on or during vacations.

5 You can with enjoy it your friends.

6 I think hiking because is an interesting activity it's relaxing and healthy.

F **Prepare a short speech about an activity you think is fun. Then practice saying it to a classmate.**

Useful words	baseball snowboarding soccer volleyball bat gloves helmet shoes net board score goal run point

Notes

_____

_____

_____

_____

_____

_____

_____

_____

TIP Remember to say what the activity is, then describe it with some details and say why it is fun.

G **Tell the class about the activity.**

Integration

H 🎧 29 **Read Sandy's blog and make notes in the table.**

Where	at school or athletics club
When	
Who	
Why	

Sandy' Blog

Wednesday May 9

I think running is an excellent sport. You can run at school or at an athletics club. You can do it after school or on the weekend. It's exciting to run against your friends. I like running because it's competitive and good for your health.

I 🎧 30 **Listen to what Mark says about running and complete the paragraph.**

I (1)_____ running is very enjoyable. You can run (2)_____ in the park or even on the (3)_____. You can do it any time you like—in the (4)_____, after school, at night or on the weekend. It's great to run with your friends or (5)_____. I think running is a good sport (6)_____ it keeps you fit.

J **Work with a classmate. Compare what Sandy and Mark said in Activities H and I.**

Sandy says that you can run at school or at an athletics club.

Mark says that you can run outside in the park or even on the street.

A **Say each word clearly.**

sport   best   skiing   park   snowy   battle

B **Say each word. Then write the number of syllables and underline the stressed syllable.**

favorite ☐   court ☐   today ☐   mountains ☐

exciting ☐   games ☐   enjoy ☐   dangerous ☐

C **Say each sentence. Then match the sentences to the stress patterns.**

1 I'm going to play computer games at home.   **a** ● ● ● ● ● ●

2 You can play it after school.   **b** ● ● ● ● ● ● ● ●

3 What else do you like playing?   **c** ● ● ● ● ● ● ● ●

4 I like basketball because it's exciting and fun.   **d** ● ● ● ● ● ●

D **Complete the dialogue about free time activities. Then practice saying it with a classmate.**

Ben: Hi. What are you doing after school today?

Me: I've got some free time, so _____.

Ben: Oh, really? I like _____, too.

Me: Which _____?

Ben: I like _____

very much. It's really great.

Me: Well, I like _____.

_____.

Review 2

E Prepare descriptions for two of the sports below that you would like to try.

Notes

_____
_____
_____
_____
_____
_____
_____
_____

surfing

skiing

snowboarding

rock climbing

Notes

_____
_____
_____
_____
_____
_____
_____
_____
_____

F Tell the class about the sports you would like to try.

Speaking Model

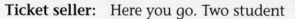

A 🎧 31 **Listen and read.**

Ticket seller:	Here you go. Two student tickets. Have a nice day at our park.
Jin-Ho:	Ah … excuse me, what time does the park close today?
Ticket seller:	Our park closes at five today.
Jin-Ho:	OK, thanks a lot.
Ticket seller:	Hey, don't forget your tickets!
Jin-Ho:	Oh! Thank you.

Jane:	Sorry to bother you, but could you tell me where the lions are?
Attendant:	Sure, no problem. Keep walking straight and turn right when you see the gift shop. The lion enclosure is really big—you can't miss it.
Jane:	Great. Thank you so much.

B **Follow the instructions.**

1 Underline the phrases that Jin-Ho and Jane say before they ask someone a question.

2 Circle two expressions that show different ways of saying "thank you."

Speaking Skill

Using polite phrases

You should be polite when you ask for help. Before you ask the question, you can use "excuse me" phrases like *Sorry to bother you.* or *Excuse me.* After someone has helped you, you should thank the person.

Speaking Practice

 **C 32 Listen and repeat. Then work with a classmate and take turns saying each sentence using the words given.**

1	What time does the park close today?	shop, center open
2	Could you tell me where the lions are?	tigers, pandas
3	Turn right when you see the gift shop.	left the gate, the snack bar
4	Great. Thank you so much.	Excellent, Wonderful

Pronunciation Focus

D 33-35 Listen and repeat.

Sounds

| five | forget |
| five | vacation |

Words

straight   right
prob·lem   bo·ther   ex·cuse
en·clo·sure

Sentences

1 Have a nice day at our park.

2 Hey, don't forget your tickets!

3 Sorry to bother you.

TIP Be aware of the sounds for the letter *f* and the letter *v*. The sound for *f* is unvoiced and the sound for *v* is voiced.

36 Listen and complete the dialogues. Then practice the dialogues with a classmate.

1 Kevin: (1)_____

_____, but

how long is the wildlife tour?

Guide: It's about an hour.

Kevin: OK, (2)_____.

2 Joan: (3)_____.

Could you tell me where the gift shop is?

Attendant: Sure, no problem. Go straight and turn

left—you can't miss it.

Joan: Great. (4)_____.

F Prepare a dialogue asking for directions in a wildlife park. Then practice the dialogue with a classmate.

kangaroos

penguins

crocodiles

monkeys

bears

gift shop
restrooms

You are
here

snack bar

ticket
office

_____

_____

_____

_____

_____

_____

_____

TIP

Remember to use "excuse me" and "thank you" when you ask for help.

G Present your dialogue to the class.

Integration

 H (37) **Listen to the dialogue and circle**
True **or** *False***.**

1	Ben bought two tickets.	(True) / False
2	Ben asked the ticket seller for a map.	True / False
3	The ticket seller probably thinks the dolphin show is good.	True / False
4	Ben did not say if he would go to see the pandas.	True / False
5	The ticket seller is not happy with Ben's second question.	True / False

 I (37) **Listen to the dialogue again and complete the information sheet.**

Animal Wonders Wildlife Park   General Information

Tickets
Adult $20
Senior $18
Student $_____
Child $12

Hours
8:30 a.m. to 7:00 p.m. every day

Guided Tours
Tour A starts at 11:00 a.m.
Tour B starts at 1:00 p.m.

Special Programs
Dolphin Show: _____ to 4:30 p.m.
Panda Show: _____ to 6:45 p.m.

 J   **Use the information from Activity I to tell the class about the wildlife park.**

Speaking Model

A 🎧 38 **Listen and read.**

Jung: Hey guys, we're doing a project about animals. Why don't we share some information? Let's start with the tiger. Do you know any facts about tigers?

Tina: Well, the tiger is a big cat and it looks fierce. It has black stripes. It lives in the jungle and it hunts for food. It likes to eat meat.

Tommy: I know the tiger usually lives alone. Also, it can be found in many parts of Asia.

Jung: Great. Now let's put all that information together.

B **Check [✓] the kinds of information Tina and Tommy give about the tiger.**

Where in the world it can be found ⬜	How it looks ⬜	Where it lives ⬜
How it gets its food ⬜	When it sleeps ⬜	What it likes to eat ⬜
What kind of animal it is ⬜	How dangerous it is ⬜	How it lives ⬜

Speaking Skill

Describing things with facts

A fact is something that is true. When talking about facts in your description, you should use the simple present tense.

Speaking Practice

C 🎧 39 **Listen and repeat. Then work with a classmate and take turns saying each sentence using the words given.**

1	The tiger is a big cat.	shark huge fish
2	It looks fierce.	cute, friendly
3	It likes to eat meat.	plants, fish
4	It can be found in many parts of Asia.	the Pacific Ocean, Australia

D 🎧 40-42 **Listen and repeat.**

Sounds		**Words**
share	sure	jun·gle A·sia
Asia	usually	to·geth·er
		u·su·al·ly in·for·ma·tion

Sentences

1 • • ● ●
    It has black stripes.

2 • • ● ●
    It lives in the jungle.

3 • • • ● ● ● ●
    I know the tiger usually lives alone.

TIP Be aware of the different sounds for the letter *s* in words like *sure* and *usually*.

E 🎧 43 **Complete the paragraph using the correct verb forms. Then listen and practice saying the paragraph with a classmate.**

The whale **(1)**_____ (be) a sea

creature. It **(2)**_____ (be) big and

gentle. It **(3)**_____ (have) smooth

skin and a big tail. It **(4)**_____ (live)

in the ocean and it **(5)**_____ (eat)

tiny plants and animals. The whale usually

(6)_____ (live) in groups.

F **Prepare some facts for a short speech about your favorite animal.**

Useful words	sea creature mammal reptile bird insect
	scary unusual beautiful ugly strong forest desert

Animal: _____

Facts: _____

_____

_____

_____

_____

_____

_____

_____

_____

TiP

Remember to use the simple present tense when you talk about facts in your descriptions.

G **Tell the class about your favorite animal.**

35

Integration

H 🎧 **44** **Read what Jason says about the crocodile and complete the table.**

The Crocodile   by Jason Yim

The crocodile is a reptile. It has rough skin and big teeth so it looks unfriendly. It eats meat and lives in rivers and lakes.

The crocodile usually lives alone. It can be found in many parts of Australia, Asia, Africa and South America.

What is it?	
What does it have?	
How does it look?	
What does it eat?	
Where does it live?	
How does it live?	
Where can it be found?	

I 🎧 **45** **Listen to what Kim says about the crocodile and complete the paragraph.**

The crocodile is a reptile, but it **(1)**_____ a lot like a dinosaur! It's fierce and scary. It **(2)**_____ a long tail and very small **(3)**_____ and feet. It lives in rivers and lakes, **(4)**_____ there are also saltwater crocodiles. The crocodile **(5)**_____ alone. It can be **(6)**_____ in rivers like the Nile and the Amazon.

J **Work with a classmate. Compare what Jason and Kim said in Activities H and I.**

Jason says that the crocodile is a reptile.

Kim says that it looks a lot like a dinosaur.

Review 3

A **Say each word clearly.**

five   Asia   sure   forget   share   vacation

B **Say each word. Then write the number of syllables and underline the stressed syllable.**

jungle ☐   together ☐   straight ☐   bother ☐

excuse ☐   information ☐   problem ☐   usually ☐

C **Say each sentence. Then match the sentences to the stress patterns.**

1 It lives in the jungle.   **a** ∙ ∙ ● ●

2 Hey, don't forget your tickets!   **b** ● ● ● ∙ ●

3 It has black stripes.   **c** ∙ ● ∙ ∙ ●

4 Sorry to bother you.   **d** ● ∙ ● ∙

D **Complete the dialogues about asking for time and directions at a park. Then practice saying them with a classmate.**

1 **Ticket seller:** OK, here are your tickets. I hope you enjoy your day at our park.

    Me: _____ .

    _____ ?

    Ticket seller: At 5.30.

    Me: _____ .

2 **Me:** _____

    _____ ?

    Attendant: Sure, no problem. Turn left and walk straight until you see the sign. The polar bear enclosure is really big, so you can't miss it.

    Me: _____ .

Prepare a short speech about one of the animals.

	Penguin	Polar bear
What is it?	bird	bear
How does it look?	cute and funny	gentle and friendly
What does it have?	small wings, feathers, long body	large legs, fur, long body
Where does it live?	ocean and land	sea, ice and land
What does it eat?	fish	seals, fish and sea birds
How does it live?	groups	alone
Where can it be found?	Southern hemisphere (Antarctica, New Zealand, Australia)	Northern hemisphere (the Arctic, Alaska, Canada)

Notes

_____

_____

_____

_____

_____

F **Tell the class about one of the animals.**

How much is this?

Speaking Model

A 🎧 46 **Listen and read.**

Dave: Excuse me. How much does this candy bar cost?

Cashier: That's 85 cents.

Dave: I'm sorry. How much did you say?

Cashier: 85 cents.

Dave: OK, I'll take it. Thanks.

Aiko: Sorry, but where can I find the potato chips?

Cashier: Over there, next to the drinks.

Aiko: Excuse me. Which drinks?

Cashier: I mean the drinks in the fridge. Just over there.

Aiko: Oh, OK. Thanks.

B **Answer the questions.**

1 What are Dave and Aiko trying to find out?

2 What do Dave and Aiko say before they ask their second questions?

Speaking Skill

Asking for clarification

When you do not hear or understand clearly what someone says, you can ask the person to say it again or give you more information. To be polite, begin by saying *Excuse me.* or *I'm sorry.*

Speaking Practice

C 🎧47 **Listen and repeat. Then work with a classmate. Take turns saying each sentence using the words given.**

1	Excuse me. How much does this candy bar cost?	ice cream, milkshake
2	I'm sorry. How much did you say?	Where, How many
3	Where can I find the potato chips?	soft drinks, candy bars
4	Excuse me. Which drinks?	shelf, box

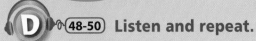
Pronunciation Focus

D 🎧48-50 **Listen and repeat.**

Sounds

potato	cent	but
does	candy	find

Words

cost   fridge   drinks
sor·ry   o·ver
po·ta·to

Sentences

1   Sorry, but where can I find the potato chips?

2   Over there, next to the drinks.

3   I mean the drinks in the fridge.

TiP Question words (*where, when, what, how much*) are usually stressed in sentences.

E 🎧 51 **Put the dialogue in the correct order. Then listen and practice the dialogue with a classmate.**

Cashier: 15 cents each. ⬭

Cashier: 15 cents each. ⬭

Bobby: Hello. How much are these chocolates? ⬭

Bobby: Excuse me. How much did you say? ⬭

Bobby: Oh, 15. Thanks. ⬭

F **Work with a classmate. Prepare two dialogues asking and answering questions at a store.**

Useful words	chocolate noodles bread soda orange juice cola under behind

Asking where something is

_____ _____

_____ _____

_____ _____

_____ _____

Asking how much something is

_____ _____

_____ _____

_____ _____

_____ _____

G **Present your dialogues to the class.**

TIP Remember to begin your dialogues politely by saying *Excuse me.* or *I'm sorry.*

Integration

H 🎧 **52** **Read the menu. Then listen and complete the dialogue.**

Menu

Soup of the Day	$2.60
Fruit and Cream Pie	$3.00
Potatoes with Broccoli and Cheese	$3.20
Country Fried Steak	$5.80
Turkey and Cheese Wraps	$4.80
Cheeseburger	$4.40
Sandwich	from $4.00

with choice of turkey, ham, roast beef or grilled chicken

Sides: Mashed Potatoes, Green Salad, Mixed Vegetables

Cindy: Excuse (1)_____.
How (2)_____ is the
grilled chicken sandwich?

Cashier: $4.60.

Cindy: I'm (3)_____. How
much (4)_____ you
say?

Cashier: $4.60.

Cindy: OK. How (5)_____
the cheeseburger with green
salad?

Cashier: That's $5.80.

Cindy: OK. I'll (6)_____
the cheeseburger with green salad and a bottle of (7)_____.

Cashier: (8)_____. That'll be $6.40.

I **Work with a classmate. Take turns asking and answering the questions.**

1   Why does Cindy ask for the price of the grilled chicken sandwich?

2   How much does the cheeseburger cost?

3   How much does the bottle of water cost?

4   What does Cindy say to show she is polite when she asks questions?

A ►🎧53 **Listen and read.**

Teacher:	Today we're going to talk about eating in or eating out. Tim, could you tell us which you like better— eating a meal at home or eating at a restaurant?
Tim:	Hm … I prefer to eat at a restaurant.
Teacher:	Really? Why's that?
Tim:	Well, it's more interesting to eat out and you can try new foods. I also like the special desserts!
Teacher:	They're all good reasons. Anything else?
Tim:	Yep. I also like that we don't need to cook. Everyone can relax more when we eat at a restaurant.

B **Answer the question and follow the instructions.**

1   What topic are they talking about?

2   Circle a word in the dialogue that means "like better."

3   Underline Tim's reasons for preferring to eat at a restaurant.

Speaking Skill

Saying what you prefer

You will sometimes be asked to choose between different things. You can first say the thing you prefer and then give some reasons to explain why you prefer it.

Speaking Practice

C 🎧 54 **Listen and repeat. Then work with a classmate and take turns saying each sentence using the words given.**

1	I prefer to eat at a restaurant.	home, the school cafeteria
2	It's more interesting to eat out.	more fun, cheaper at a restaurant, at home
3	You can try new foods.	different things, many dishes
4	I also like the special desserts!	starters, drinks

Pronunciation Focus

D 🎧 55-57 **Listen and repeat.**

Sounds

reason	restaurant	relax
like	meal	relax

Words

rea·son   pre·fer   re·lax   des·sert
res·tau·rant
in·ter·est·ing

Sentences

1 They're all good reasons. Anything else?

2 I also like that we don't need to cook.

3 Everyone can relax more.

TIP In two-syllable words that begin with *pre*, *re* or *de*, the stress is often on the second syllable.

58 Complete the paragraph using the words from the box. Then listen and practice saying the paragraph with a classmate.

comfortable   food   together   great   makes   home

I prefer to eat at (1)_____. It's more (2)_____ and I can eat healthier (3)_____. My mom is a (4)_____ cook. I love the special vegetarian dishes she (5)_____. It's really good that we can enjoy time (6)_____ when we eat at home.

 Prepare a short speech explaining whether you prefer to eat out or at home.

Useful words quiet noisy busy friendly delicious simple choices

Notes

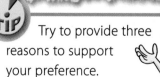 Try to provide three reasons to support your preference.

 Tell the class about your preference.

Integration

H 🎧 59 **Read about Kate's preference.**

I prefer to have the TV off while I'm eating. It's quieter and you can talk. I also like that the family can enjoy each other's company — not the sound of the television. Sometimes when I'm eating alone, I can have the chance to think quietly.

I 🎧 60 **Listen to Samuel giving his preference and complete the paragraph.**

I prefer to have the TV on when I **(1)**_____.
It's boring when the TV is **(2)**_____. I like
the **(3)**_____ to watch my favorite dramas
while I'm **(4)**_____. I also **(5)**_____
watching **(6)**_____ shows.

J **Work with a classmate. Compare what Kate and Samuel said in Activities H and I.**

Kate says that she prefers to have the TV off while she's eating.

Samuel says that he prefers to have the TV on when he eats.

46

A Say each word clearly.

cent   reason   relax   potato   find   restaurant

B Say each word. Then write the number of syllables and underline the stressed syllable.

fridge ☐   reason ☐   dessert ☐   interesting ☐

potato ☐   sorry ☐   relax ☐   over ☐

C Say each sentence. Then match the sentences to the stress patterns.

1 I also like that we don't need to cook.   **a** ● ● ● ● ● ● ● ● ●

2 Sorry, but where can I find the potato chips?   **b** ● ● ● ● ● ● ● ●

3 Over there, next to the drinks.   **c** ● ● ● ● ● ● ●

4 They're all good reasons. Anything else?   **d** ● ● ● ● ● ● ● ●

D Complete the dialogues about shopping at a store. Then practice saying them with a classmate.

1 Me: _____?

Cashier: Over there, behind the boxes.

Me: _____. _____?

Cashier: Over there. Behind the big red boxes. You can't miss them!

2 Me: _____. _____

_____?

Cashier: That's 55 cents.

Me: _____. _____?

Cashier: 55 cents.

Me: _____.

47

 Look at the two topics. Choose your preferences and give reasons for each of them. Then ask a classmate.

Do you prefer watching DVDs or going to the movie theater?

Me:

Preference: _____

Reasons: _____

_____

Classmate:

Preference: _____

Reasons: _____

_____

Do you prefer indoor or outdoor sports?

Me:

Preference: _____

Reasons: _____

_____

Classmate:

Preference: _____

Reasons: _____

_____

 Tell the class about your classmate's preferences.

Vacation Plans

Speaking Model

A 🎧 61 **Listen and read.**

Shin: Summer vacation's coming up. What are your plans?

Amy: Hm … We haven't made any plans yet. Has your family?

Shin: Yep. We're going to the beach. I can't wait!

Amy: Oh, I'm so jealous! What'll you do while you're there?

Shin: I'll go swimming and maybe learn how to surf.

Amy: That'd be so fun! I'd love to learn how to surf.

Shin: We're going to be there for two weeks. I hope that's enough time for me to learn.

B **Follow the instruction and answer the question.**

1 Circle all the words in the dialogue that use an apostrophe (').

2 What expression shows that Shin is excited about his vacation plan?

Speaking Skill

Using contractions

When people talk in conversation, they often join small common words together. These are called contractions.

| it is = it's | they are = they're | do not = don't |
| I am = I'm | you will = you'll | that would = that'd |

Speaking Practice

 **Listen and repeat. Then work with a classmate and take turns saying each sentence using the words given.**

1	Summer vacation's coming up.	The long weekend, Winter vacation
2	We're going to the beach. I can't wait!	Europe, a resort
3	I'll go swimming.	skiing, shopping
4	I'd love to learn how to surf.	swim, dive

Pronunciation Focus

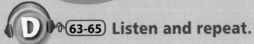 **Listen and repeat.**

Sounds

teacher   beach
jealous   dangerous

Words

love   surf   wait
jea·lous   sum·mer   may·be
va·ca·tion   fam·i·ly

Sentences

1 What'll you do while you're there?

2 We're going to be there for two weeks.

3 Oh, I'm so jealous!

TIP We say the same sound for the letters *j* and *g* in words like *jealous* and *dangerous*.

E 🎧 66 **Change the underlined words to contracted forms. Then listen and practice the dialogue with a classmate.**

Nancy: Summer ① <u>vacation is</u> coming up. Do you have any plans?

Daniel: Hm … I ② <u>have not</u> made any plans yet. Have you?

Nancy: Yep. ③ <u>We are</u> going to go camping in the mountains. I ④ <u>cannot</u> wait!

Daniel: Oh, ⑤ <u>I am</u> so jealous! ⑥ <u>What will</u> you do while ⑦ <u>you are</u> there?

Nancy: I hope ⑧ <u>I will</u> get to go hiking and rock climbing.

Daniel: ⑨ <u>That would</u> be so fun! ⑩ <u>I would</u> love to learn how to rock climb.

1   *vacation's*
2
3
4
5
6
7
8
9
10

F **Prepare a dialogue with a classmate talking about your summer vacation plans.**

Useful words   countryside   canoeing   diving   sightseeing   make friends

G **Present your dialogue to the class.**

Integration

H **Write your answers. Then ask two classmates the same questions and write their answers.**

1 Where would you like to go on vacation?

_____

_____

2 What would you do there?

_____

_____

3 How long would you go there for?

_____

_____

Name: _____

1 _____

_____

2 _____

_____

3 _____

_____

Name: _____

1 _____

_____

2 _____

_____

3 _____

_____

I **Tell the class about your classmates' vacations.**

Speaking Model

A 🎧 67 **Listen and read.**

Let me tell you what happened during summer vacation.

I went camping with my family. On the first day, we went hiking near the campsite. We reached the top of a high mountain. The view was really beautiful.

On the way back, I saw something shiny buried in the ground. It looked like a huge ring. My dad dug it out. It was an old bronze jar! We were very surprised.

When we got back, we decided to take it to a museum. They were happy because the jar was hundreds of years old.

B **Follow the instructions.**

1 Circle all the words in the story that show events happened in the past.

2 Underline sentences that show how people felt.

Speaking Skill

Telling a story

To tell a story well, you should

- talk about events in the order they happened.
- use past tense to show things happened in the past.
- use descriptions to show how people felt or what things looked like.

Speaking Practice

C 🎧 **68** **Listen and repeat. Then work with a classmate and take turns saying each sentence using the words given.**

1	On the first day, we went hiking.	Wednesday, the weekend camping, surfing
2	I saw something shiny.	He, She colorful, strange
3	It looked like a huge ring.	an old map, a big coin
4	We were very surprised.	They, All of us happy, glad

D 🎧 **69-71** **Listen and repeat.**

Sounds

summer	saw	decided
surprised	museum	bronze

Words

saw   reached
hik·ing   sur·prised
de·cid·ed   mu·se·um

Sentences

1 I went camping with my family.

2 My dad dug it out.

3 We decided to take it to a museum.

TIP
When we tell a story, action words like *went*, *dug* and *decided* are usually stressed.

54

E 72 **Put the sentences in the correct order. Then listen and tell the story to a classmate.**

On the way down, I saw a little girl sitting on the ground crying. She looked like she was lost. ☐

On the first day, we all went skiing. There were many people on the slopes. ☐

I took her back down the mountain with me. ☐

I went to the mountains with my family during winter vacation. ☐

I was very excited. I went to the highest slope. ☐

After searching for a while, I found the girl's mom. She was very happy! ☐

F **Look at the pictures and prepare a story about them. Then practice telling the story to a classmate.**

Useful words surfing far wave fin shark dolphin lead shore

Notes

_____

_____

_____

_____

_____

TIP Make sure you use the past tense form of the verbs in your story.

G **Tell your story to the class.**

 Integration

 H 🎧 73 **Read the paragraph.**

Mary went to New York City with her family during winter vacation. On the first day, they all went to see the Empire State Building. They took a taxi. It was a short ride. They went up to the top of the building to take photographs. They were amazed to see so many tall buildings from above.

 I 🎧 74 **Listen and complete the paragraph.**

Mike went to London with his family during

(1)_____ vacation. On the (2)_____

day, they wanted to go to the British Museum. They decided

to take the Tube there. It was a (3)_____ ride.

When they (4)_____ arrived at the museum,

they found it was (5)_____ that day! Everyone

was disappointed. They went shopping and had a nice

dinner instead.

J **Work with a classmate. Complete the table by comparing the two paragraphs in Activities H and I.**

	Mary	Mike
City / Place to go	New York City / Empire State Building	
Transport		
Length of the ride		
Things they did		
Their feelings		

A Say each word clearly.

beach   museum   surprised   dangerous   bronze   jealous

B Say each word. Then write the number of syllables and underline the stressed syllable.

family ☐   reached ☐   decided ☐   jealous ☐

museum ☐   vacation ☐   surprised ☐   surf ☐

C Say each sentence. Then match the sentences to the stress patterns.

1   We're going to be there for two weeks.   a   ● ● ● ● ● ● ●

2   What'll you do while you're there?   b   ● ● ● ● ● ● ● ●

3   We decided to take it to a museum.   c   ● ● ● ● ● ● ● ●

4   I went camping with my family.   d   ● ● ● ● ● ●

D Complete the dialogue about your vacation plans. Then practice saying it with a classmate.

Me: _____

_____?

Jenny: Um … We haven't made any plans yet. Has your family?

Me: _____

_____!

Jenny: Oh, I'm so jealous! What'll you do while you're there?

Me: _____.

Jenny: That'd be so fun! I'd love to do that, too.

E Look at the six pictures. Then prepare a story about them.

1. picnic / in the woods

2. ask / go for a walk

3. hungry / peanuts

4. gets dark / lost / scared

5. shells / path / follow

6. happy / parents

Notes

_____

_____

_____

_____

_____

_____

_____

_____

F Tell your story to the class.

Computer Games

Speaking Model

A 🎧 75 **Listen and read.**

Ling:	Hey, this game's really hard! I'm stuck. What should I do?
Hyun-Ki:	Go up.
Ling:	Up? Up where? I don't understand!
Hyun-Ki:	Up the stairs. You need to go up the stairs.
Ling:	Stairs? What stairs?
Hyun-Ki:	They're hidden behind the curtain. Look behind the curtain.
Ling:	Which curtain? There are three different ones!
Hyun-Ki:	Oh, sorry—the green curtain. Look behind there and you'll find some secret stairs. Climb the stairs and you'll get to the secret room.

B **Follow the instruction and answer the questions.**

1 Underline the instructions Hyun-Ki gives to Ling.

2 Which instructions are not very clear to Ling?

3 Why did Ling repeat some of the words Hyun-Ki said?

Speaking Skill

Giving instructions

Instructions tell us how to do something. Helpful instructions allow us to do things quicker or better. Giving or getting instructions involves

• saying where, why, how or when to do something.
• giving information about what comes next.
• asking questions to get more information when instructions are not clear.

Speaking Practice

C 🎧 76 **Listen and repeat. Then work with a classmate. Take turns saying each sentence using the words given.**

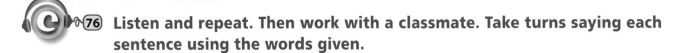

1	Up where? I don't understand!	Down where, Above what
2	You need to go up the stairs.	go down, fly above hill, tower
3	Which curtain? There are three different ones!	box, door four, five
4	Look behind there and you'll find some secret stairs.	ahead, under the chair the ring, the sword

Pronunciation Focus

D 🎧 77-79 **Listen and repeat.**

Sounds

climb   plan
green   friend

Words

need   stuck
se·cret   cur·tain
un·der·stand   dif·fer·ent

Sentences

1   Hey, this game's really hard!

2   I'm stuck. What should I do?

3   Look behind the curtain.

TIP

When we use verbs with prepositions (*look behind, go up*) in instructions, the prepositions are usually stressed.

E 🎧80 Put the dialogue in the correct order. Then listen and practice the dialogue with a classmate.

Alan

Hey, this game's difficult! What should I do? `1`

Target? What target?

Which river? There are two!

Down? Down where? I don't understand!

Jeff

The target next to the river.

Down into the valley. You need to fly down into the valley to find the target.

Fly down.

The river on the right. Fly down there and you'll see the target. `8`

F Work with a classmate. Prepare a dialogue about giving instructions on how to play the computer game.

G Present your dialogue to the class.

> **TIP** When instructions are not clear, you can ask questions beginning with *where*, *what* and *which* to get more information.

Integration

H (81-82) **Read the notice. Then listen and complete the dialogue.**

Dragon Internet Cafe

Please get your access code from the payment counter.

No food or drinks at the computers.

Hours: 8 a.m.–11 p.m.

Terry: I'm sorry to (1)_____ you, but could you (2)_____ me?

Amy: Yes, sure.

Terry: (3)_____ the payment counter? I want to

get an access code.

Amy: Over (4)_____.

Terry: Over (5)_____?

Amy: There. Next to the big blue door.

Terry: Thanks. Is there somewhere I can get

something to eat?

Amy: Yeah, (6)_____ a snack bar.

Terry: Snack bar? Where's that?

Amy: It's (7)_____ the corner.

Terry: Oh, I see. Thanks for (8)_____ help.

I **Work with a classmate. Take turns asking and answering the questions.**

1 What does Terry want to get?

2 Where is the payment counter?

3 Where can Terry get something to eat?

4 Why can't Terry see the snack bar?

Online Chatting

Speaking Model

A 🎧 83 **Listen and read.**

Teacher: OK, we're going to debate whether online chatting is good or bad for us. We'll start with you, David. Are you for or against online chatting?

David: Well, online chatting is good, I think. It's good for making friends. Maybe it helps us relax, too.

Teacher: Thank you, David. Now Ann, your turn.

Ann: I'm against online chatting. First, you can't be sure who you're talking to. Second, it's easy to spend too much time chatting online. Third, it's not as natural as talking face to face.

B **Answer the questions.**

1 Does David's first line clearly say he is for or against online chatting?

2 Who says his/her ideas in better order? Why?

3 Who speaks more clearly and confidently, David or Ann?

Speaking Skill

Expressing opinions in a debate

Debating is a formal way for people to discuss and to express their ideas and opinions on something. To debate well, you need to

- be for (agree with) or against (disagree with) the topic.
- say your reasons in a clear order (*first, second, third*).
- speak clearly and confidently to make listeners believe you are right.

Speaking Practice

 84 **Listen and repeat. Then work with a classmate and take turns saying each sentence using the words given.**

1	It's good for making friends.	sharing ideas, getting information
2	It helps us relax.	learn more
3	It's easy to spend too much time chatting online.	bad, unhealthy playing computer games
4	It's not as natural as talking face to face.	good, easy chatting on the phone

Pronunciation Focus

D 85-87 **Listen and repeat.**

Sounds

think	third
the	whether

Words

good   bad
de·bate   be·cause
nat·u·ral

Sentences

1 Are you for or against online chatting?

2 Well, online chatting is good, I think.

3 I'm against online chatting.

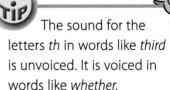

TIP

The sound for the letters *th* in words like *third* is unvoiced. It is voiced in words like *whether*.

88 **Check [✓] if each sentence is for or against the topic. Then listen and practice saying the sentences with a classmate.**

The Internet is the best tool for learning.

		For	Against
1	We can find information easily on the Internet.	☐	☐
2	Not all the information on the Internet is correct.	☐	☐
3	We get many useless junk emails.	☐	☐
4	The Internet is good for downloading pictures.	☐	☐
5	Email helps us to share information with people.	☐	☐
6	Viruses can destroy the information on our computers.	☐	☐

F **Work with a classmate. Decide if you are for or against the topic. Then write three supporting reasons.**

Online shopping is the best way to shop.

Useful words	time-saving quick lose money shopping malls
	safe relaxing comfortable

For ☐   Against ☐

Reasons:

- _____
  _____

- _____
  _____

- _____
  _____

G **Debate the topic with another pair of classmates.**

 (89) Read what Penny says about the topic.

All classrooms should have computers.

I think that all classrooms should have computers. First, we can use them to find information for projects quickly. Second, we can type up stories and diaries and save them easily. Third, teachers can use the computers to help explain difficult topics, so that we can learn more.

 (90) Listen and complete Yong's speech.

Yes, I **(1)**_____ think that all classrooms should have computers. **(2)**_____, we can use a search engine to find information **(3)**_____. Second, when we type on the computer, it's **(4)**_____ to check spelling and correct mistakes. **(5)**_____, we save **(6)**_____ when we answer questions on the computer.

J Work with a classmate. Compare Penny's and Yong's opinions.

Penny thinks that we can use computers to find information for projects quickly.

Yong thinks that we can use a search engine to find information easily.

A **Say each word clearly.**

think   green   whether   friend   third   plan

B **Say each word. Then write the number of syllables and underline the stressed syllable.**

debate ☐   stuck ☐   natural ☐   understand ☐

because ☐   good ☐   curtain ☐   different ☐

C **Say each sentence. Then match the sentences to the stress patterns.**

1   Look behind the curtain.   a   ● ● · ● · ●

2   I'm stuck. What should I do?   b   · ● ● ●

3   Online chatting is good, I think.   c   · ● ● ● · ●

4   I'm against chatting online.   d   · ● · ●

D **Complete the dialogue about playing a computer game. Then practice saying it with a classmate.**

Me: Hey, this game's really hard! I'm stuck. _____?

David: Go inside.

Me: _____? _____?

_____!

David: Inside the cave. You need to go inside the cave to find the key.

Me: _____? _____?

David: Look under the rock.

Me: _____? _____

_____!

David: The white rock. Look under there and you'll find the key.

Review
6

 Work with a classmate. Decide if you are for or against the topic and write three supporting reasons.

Emails are better than letters.

Reasons for:

1 _____

_____

2 _____

_____

3 _____

_____

Reasons against:

1 _____

_____

2 _____

_____

3 _____

_____

 Debate the topic with another pair of classmates.

Pronunciation

Sounds

Unit					CD Track	Page
1	/m/	name	meet	from	4	p. 10
	/n/	name	nice	been		
	/ŋ/	long	studying			
2	/k/	kind	look	carefully	10	p. 14
	/g/	girl	big	guess		
3	/p/	park	power		17	p. 20
	/b/	best	battle			
4	/sk/	skiing			25	p. 24
	/sp/	sport				
	/sn/	snowy				
5	/f/	five	forget		33	p. 30
	/v/	five	vacation			
6	/ʃ/	share	sure		40	p. 34
	/ʒ/	Asia	usually			
7	/t/	potato	cent	but	48	p. 40
	/d/	does	candy	find		
8	/r/	reason	restaurant	relax	55	p. 44
	/l/	like	meal	relax		
9	/tʃ/	teacher	beach		63	p. 50
	/dʒ/	jealous	dangerous			
10	/s/	summer	saw	decided	69	p. 54
	/z/	surprised	museum	bronze		
11	/kl/	climb			77	p. 60
	/pl/	plan				
	/gr/	green				
	/fr/	friend				
12	/θ/	think	third		85	p. 64
	/ð/	the	whether			

Words

One Syllable

	CD Track	Page
bad	86	p. 64
cost	49	p. 40
court	26	p. 24
drinks	49	p. 40
free	18	p. 20
fridge	49	p. 40
games	18	p. 20
good	86	p. 64
great	26	p. 24
love	64	p. 50
man	11	p. 14
meet	5	p. 10
my	5	p. 10
need	78	p. 60
nice	5	p. 10
pleased	11	p. 14
reached	70	p. 54
right	34	p. 30
room	11	p. 14
saw	70	p. 54
straight	34	p. 30
stuck	78	p. 60
surf	64	p. 50
time	18	p. 20
wait	64	p. 50

Two Syllables

	CD Track	Page
A·sia	41	p. 34
be·cause	86	p. 64
bo·ther	34	p. 30
cen·ter	26	p. 24
cur·tain	78	p. 60
de·bate	86	p. 64
des·sert	56	p. 44
en·joy	18	p. 20
Eng·lish	5	p. 10
ex·cuse	34	p. 30
hik·ing	70	p. 54
jea·lous	64	p. 50
jun·gle	41	p. 34
list·en	11	p. 14
may·be	64	p. 50
moun·tains	26	p. 24
o·ver	49	p. 40
play·ing	18	p. 20
pre·fer	56	p. 44
prob·lem	34	p. 30
rea·son	56	p. 44
real·ly	5	p. 10
re·lax	56	p. 44
se·cret	78	p. 60
sor·ry	49	p. 40
sum·mer	64	p. 50
sur·prised	70	p. 54
teach·er	11	p. 14
to·day	18	p. 20

Three Syllables

	CD Track	Page
care·ful·ly	11	p. 14
com·put·er	18	p. 20
dan·ger·ous	26	p. 24
de·cid·ed	70	p. 54
dif·fer·ent	78	p. 60
en·clo·sure	34	p. 30
ex·cit·ing	26	p. 24
fam·i·ly	64	p. 50
fa·vo·rite	18	p. 20
I·tal·y	5	p. 10
mu·se·um	70	p. 54
nat·u·ral	86	p. 64
po·ta·to	49	p. 40
res·tau·rant	56	p. 44
stud·y·ing	5	p. 10
to·geth·er	41	p. 34
un·der·stand	78	p. 60
u·ni·form	11	p. 14
va·ca·tion	64	p. 50

Four Syllables

	CD Track	Page
in·for·ma·tion	41	p. 34
in·ter·est·ing	56	p. 44
u·su·al·ly	41	p. 34

Sentences

Unit		CD Track	Page
1	Nice to meet you, too. Where are you from? I've been at this school for only two weeks.	6	p. 10
2	There are six students. They're not wearing uniforms. All of the students look kind of serious.	12	p. 14
3	I'm going to play computer games at home. What else do you like playing? Wow, that sounds great.	19	p. 20
4	It's a team sport. You can play it after school. I like basketball because it's exciting and fun.	27	p. 24
5	Have a nice day at our park. Hey, don't forget your tickets! Sorry to bother you.	35	p. 30
6	It has black stripes. It lives in the jungle. I know the tiger usually lives alone.	42	p. 34